DINOSAURS!

ALLOSAURUS
AND OTHER DINOSAURS AND REPTILES FROM
THE UPPER JURASSIC

by
David West

Gareth Stevens
Publishing

Please visit our website, www.garethstevens.com.
For a free color catalog of all our high-quality books,
call toll free 1-800-542-2595 or fax 1-877-542-2596.

Library of Congress Cataloging-in-Publication Data

West, David, 1956-
Allosaurus and other dinosaurs and reptiles from the upper Jurassic / David West.
p. cm. — (Dinosaurs!)
Includes index.
ISBN 978-1-4339-6705-4 (pbk.)
ISBN 978-1-4339-6706-1 (6-pack)
ISBN 978-1-4339-6704-7 (library binding)
1. Allosaurus—Juvenile literature. 2. Dinosaurs—Juvenile literature. I. Title.
QE862.S3W464 2012
567.9—dc23
2011034332

First Edition

Published in 2012 by
Gareth Stevens Publishing
111 East 14th Street, Suite 349
New York, NY 10003

Designed by David West Books

Special thanks to Dr Ron Blakey for the map on page 4

Printed in China

CPSIA compliance information: Batch #DW12GS: For further information contact Gareth Stevens, New York, New York at 1-800-542-2595.

Contents

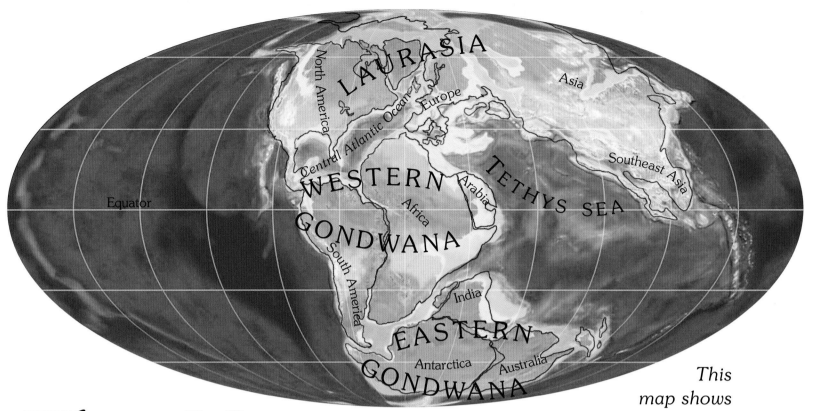

This map shows what the world looked like around 150 million years ago.

The Upper Jurassic Period

The continents continued to move apart as a new sea, the Central Atlantic Ocean, developed between North America and Africa. The southern continent began to split into Western Gondwana and Eastern Gondwana. The interior of Pangaea became less dry and less seasonal. Sea levels remained high and flooded large areas of Europe, which created a mass of small islands.

*Dinosaurs lived throughout the Mesozoic Era, which is divided into three periods, shown here. It is sometimes called the Age of Reptiles. Dinosaurs first appeared in the Upper Triassic period and died out during a **mass extinction event** 65 million years ago.*

The first birds appeared.

Large marine reptiles swam in the oceans.

LIFE DURING THE UPPER JURASSIC

This last period of the Jurassic saw dinosaurs reach enormous sizes. These were the **sauropods**, and they existed on every continent. As the **herbivores** grew bigger, so did the predators, the most famous being *Allosaurus*. It was also during this period that the first birds appeared, although they looked very different from the birds we know today. At the end of the Upper Jurassic period, there was a minor mass extinction. It was not as severe as the one at the end of the Triassic. Some of the **stegosaurids** died out, as did many types of **ammonites** and **bivalves** and all but one type of **ichthyosaur**. No one knows what caused this extinction.

227	200	180	159	144		98		65 Millions of years ago (mya)
	Upper	Lower	Middle	Upper	Lower		Upper	
TRIASSIC		JURASSIC			CRETACEOUS			

5

Land of the Giants

During the Upper Jurassic period, sauropods grew larger and became more specialized in their feeding habits. In what is today North America, many of these giants roamed the landscape, feeding off the ferns, **cycads**, and branches of conifers such as the giant redwoods.

One of the most common sauropods of this time was *Camarasaurus*. These dinosaurs had air pockets in their spine that were connected to their lungs. This allowed them to increase the amount of air required

In a redwood forest, an adult Camarasaurus *(1)* turns to face a *Saurophaganax (2),* which is chasing after **juvenile** Camarasauruses *along a shallow river. A* Brachiosaurus *(3)* looks on from the other bank. Apatosauruses *(4)* feed on ferns in the distance.

for their massive bodies. Living alongside *Camarasaurus* were *Brachiosaurus* and *Apatosaurus*. *Brachiosaurus* was one of the largest dinosaurs, and it could graze on branches 29.5 feet (9 m) off the ground. *Apatosaurus* was a long-tailed sauropod similar to *Diplodocus* (see pages 8–9). **Preying** on the smaller juveniles of these giants was a large **allosaurid** called *Saurophaganax*.

Camarasaurus grew up to 75 feet (23 m) long and weighed around 51.8 tons (47 metric tons).

2

3

Tail Whips and Spikes

One type of giant sauropod grew to enormous lengths. This was *Diplodocus*. The tail was longer than the rest of its body and could be as long as 69 feet (21 m)! **Paleontologists** think its tail was used like a whip to strike **predators** such as *Torvosaurus* and *Allosaurus*.

Torvosaurus means "Savage Lizard," and along with *Allosaurus* (see pages 10–11) and *Saurophaganax,* it was the largest predator of its day. At a whopping 30 feet (9.0 m) in length, with a weight of about

A herd of Diplodocuses (1) *fend off an attack from a* Torvosaurus (2) *by using their whip-like tails. In the foreground, a* Ceratosaurus (3) *approaches a* Stegosaurus (4) *with one eye on its sharp tail spikes.*

2.15 tons (1.95 metric tons), this mighty **carnivore** was a serious threat to the large sauropods of the Upper Jurassic. Another large meat eater was *Ceratosaurus*. From its head grew three horn-like crests, which give it its name, "Horn Lizard." Fossil evidence shows that it preyed on *Stegosaurus*. This herbivore was no easy meal, as it too had a sting in its tail.

Diplodocus grew up to 115 feet (35 m) long and weighed around 50 tons (45.4 metric tons).

Upper Jurassic
150 mya
North America

Allosaurus

In the forests and plains of the Upper Jurassic 150 million years ago, in what is now North America, a large two-legged predator preyed on herbivores. Its name was *Allosaurus*, and it was one of the largest and most ferocious hunters of its time.

Allosaurus was a hunter of large animals. Its arms were suited for both grasping prey at a distance and clutching it close. Its prey would have included the sauropods *Apatosaurus*, *Brachiosaurus*, *Camarasaurus*,

An Ornitholestes (1) *with a lizard watches an* Allosaurus (2) *feeding on a* Dryosaurus (3). Palaeopteryxes (4) *run overhead while a* Gargoyleosaurus (5) *munches on low-lying plants. A pair of* Camptosauruses (6) *feed, unaware of the danger close by.*

and *Diplodocus* as well as smaller dinosaurs such as *Stegosaurus,* *Camptosaurus,* and *Dryosaurus.* Even the armored *Gargoyleosaurus* may have got its attention, although this spiky dinosaur might have been too tough a nut to crack. Living alongside were small hunters such as *Ornitholestes.* Growing to 6.8 feet (2.1 m), this small **theropod** preyed on lizards, frogs, and other little animals.

Allosaurus grew to 28 feet (8.5 m) long and weighed, at a guess, up to 2.5 tons (2.3 metric tons).

1

High–Low Feeders

Discovered by a South American shepherd out looking for his sheep, the **fossil** remains of *Brachytrachelopan* proved to be a rare find. Paleontologists were stunned to discover that this dinosaur did not conform to the long-necked, long-tailed proportions of other sauropods.

Brachytrachelopan, which means "short-necked shepherd," had the shortest neck of all sauropods. Scientists have suggested that these sauropods evolved with shorter necks to feed on low-lying vegetation

In a Gondwanan landscape, a herd of Brachytrachelopans (1) *feed on low-lying ferns and cycads while a pair of* Tehuelchesauruses (2) *browse on the upper branches of some monkey puzzle trees.*

such as ferns and cycads. *Brachytrachelopan* was small for a sauropod and probably lived in herds. Its low-level feeding habits would not have conflicted with larger sauropods living at the same time, such as *Tehuelchesaurus*. These long-necked dinosaurs would have fed on the tall pine trees using their needle-like teeth to strip the leaves off the branches.

Brachytrachelopan grew to 33 feet (10 m) long and weighed 5 tons (4.5 metric tons).

13

Ocean Hunters

The Upper Jurassic oceans teemed with sea life. Many of the hunters were reptiles that spent their entire lives at sea, rising to the surface to breathe air before plunging into the depths to catch their prey.

Many types of ichthyosaurs inhabited the shallow seas and the deep oceans. Ichthyosaurs such as *Brachypterygius* and the larger *Caypullisaurus* used their large eyes to hunt in the dark depths of the ocean for squid. They looked very similar to today's dolphins, and like

14

A Dakosaurus (1) *harasses a* Caypullisaurus (2) *as it returns to the surface for air. A pair of* Brachypterygius (3) *swim at speed from a* Liopleurodon (4). *In the foreground, the ever-present ammonites (5) glide through the Upper Jurassic ocean.*

them, these marine reptiles also gave birth to live young at sea. Large **plesiosaurs** like *Liopleurodon* lived in the oceans preying on ichthyosaurs and other plesiosaurs. Hunting alongside them was a ferocious marine **crocodilian** called *Dakosaurus*. It had a head like a dinosaur with jaws filled with large, sharp, serrated teeth. It would tear chunks out of any prey slow enough to be caught.

Dakosaurus grew up to 13 feet (4 m) long and weighed 1,500 pounds (681 kg).

Out of Africa

Fossils from the Upper Jurassic continent of Africa show that many of the dinosaurs of the North American continent also lived in Africa. These include the sauropod *Brachiosaurus* and the theropods *Allosaurus* and *Ceratosaurus*.

Ceratosaurus was 20 feet (6 m) long and had a long, flexible body with a deep tail shaped like that of a crocodilian, making it a good swimmer. Studies suggested that *Ceratosaurus* hunted **aquatic** prey,

A Kentrosaurus (1) *feeds on ferns and cycads on the edge of a river near the coast. It is undisturbed by a* Ceratosaurus (2) *chasing an* Elaphrosaurus (3) *across the river while* Pterodactyluses (4) *fly overhead.*

such as fish and crocodiles, although it fed on large dinosaurs as well. Other carnivorous theropods such as *Elaphrosaurus* might also have been attacked by *Ceratosaurus*. Plant eaters such as *Kentrosaurus* may have been attacked as well. But, like the larger *Stegosaurus*, *Kentrosaurus* had a tail full of spikes that could be swung in a wide arc at over 31 mph (50 km/h), causing severe injury.

Kentrosaurus was about 15 feet (4.6 m) long and weighed around 1.2 tons (1.1 metric tons).

4

1

African Giants

Hunting the herds of large sauropods of the African Upper Jurassic was the giant of theropods, *Allosaurus*. Using stealth and ambush, this heavyweight predator would attack the old, young, and sick. A large, healthy sauropod would be too dangerous even for an *Allosaurus*.

Many types of sauropods lived in herds in what is today Africa. One of the largest of its day was *Giraffatitan,* which weighed in at a massive 41 tons (37 metric tons). It would probably have needed to eat more

An Allosaurus (1) *prowls close to a herd of* Dicraeosauruses (2) *during a rainstorm. In the distance, a juvenile* Giraffatitan (3) *browses on the branches of a pine tree. A herd of* Tornieria (4) *move in to compete for the lush feeding grounds.*

than 400 pounds (182 kg) of food per day. Living alongside was *Tornieria*, a giant, long-tailed, plant-eating dinosaur closely related to the better-known *Diplodocus* (see pages 8–9). Competing for food was a smaller sauropod called *Dicraeosaurus*. It was named after the two rows of spines down its back. This sauropod had a shorter neck than its companions and probably browsed on lower vegetation.

Dicraeosaurus was about 41 feet (12.5 m) long and would have weighed around 11 tons (10 metric tons).

Small World

During the Jurassic period, parts of Europe were swamped by the sea, leaving a scattering of islands. Dinosaurs became isolated on these small worlds, where food sources were limited. Paleontologists have found evidence that dinosaurs on these islands became smaller and evolved into dwarf species.

Europasaurus, which was a sauropod, was only 20 feet (6 m) long. It evolved into a dwarf species quite quickly as the island it lived on,

A group of Europasauruses (1) *wade ashore one of the many islands that made up Europe during the Upper Jurassic.* A group of Compsognathuses (2) *hunt the shore for food while a pair of* Juravenators (3) *chase after a couple of* Archaeopteryxes (4).

which was less than 772 square miles (2,000 sq km), would not have possessed enough food for a population of large sauropods. Even the predators on these tiny islands were small. Both *Juravenator* and *Compsognathus* were probably the top predators, but they were far too small to worry *Europasaurus*. **Pterosaurs** like *Rhamphorhynchus* and early birds like *Archaeopteryx* were also found on these islands.

Juravenator was about 30 inches (75 cm) long and weighed up to 3.3 pounds (1.5 kg).

Water Margins

On the bigger islands and mainland of Upper Jurassic Europe roamed some of the larger dinosaurs. Water, such as swamps, lakes, and rivers, attracted many of these dinosaurs as it was here that food was plentiful.

Plant-eating dinosaurs such as *Dacentrurus* fed on cycads and ferns growing near the water's edge. These plated dinosaurs were similar in shape to *Stegosaurus* but had more spines along their tail. Small plant eaters like the **iguanodont** *Draconyx* might visit the water's margin to

A *flock of* Pterodactyluses (1) *fly above the edge of a lake. They are joined by three* Rhamphorhynchuses (2). *Below them, a* Dacentrurus (3) *feeds on cycads as a* Goniopholis (4) *swims close by. Stalking it is a* Ceratosaurus (5), *watched by nervous* Draconyxes (6).

drink. If attacked, they could run on two legs, using speed to escape predators such as *Ceratosaurus*. This carnivorous predator hunted the rivers and shallow lakes for fish and crocodilians such as *Goniopholis*. The air above was alive with flying reptiles such as the long-tailed *Rhamphorhynchus* and the more modern, short-tailed *Pterodactylus*.

Pterodactylus grew up to 5 feet (1.5 m) long and weighed around 5 pounds (2.3 kg).

23

European Giants

Wandering the plains and forests of the Upper Jurassic European islands were herds of sauropods feeding on pines, cycads, and ferns. These giants grew to enormous sizes like those on the North American continent. As always, there were large predators that hunted the young and the sick.

Grazing on tall pines was *Lusotitan*, a large sauropod, 82 feet (25 m) long, resembling *Brachiosaurus*. Feeding alongside were herds of

A Stegosaurus (1) *bellows and swishes its spiked tail in defense against an attack by a* Metriacanthosaurus (2). *A pair of close-by* Lusotitans (3) *call out a warning to other dinosaurs as a group of* Dinheirosauruses (4) *stroll past in the distance.*

Dinheirosauruses. Once thought to be *Diplodocuses*, these long-tailed sauropods evolved into a separate family as they became isolated on islands. Hunting these giant dinosaurs was a large carnivorous theropod called *Metriacanthosaurus*. It may well have also preyed on *Stegosaurus*.

Stegosaurus was around 29.5 feet (9 m) in length and weighed about 3.5 tons (3.2 metric tons).

2

3

Asian Giants

Upper Jurassic Asia was home to a dinosaur with one of the longest necks of any animal to roam the planet. Its name was *Mamenchisaurus,* and it was a giant sauropod. Its neck made up over half its total length of 82 feet (25 m).

The long neck of *Mamenchisaurus* allowed it to eat the tough leaves of the tallest trees. Other sauropods could not reach as high and therefore did not compete for the same food source. Its massive size

A pair of Yangchuanosauruses (1) *approach a water hole in a semiarid region. A flock of* Huanhepteruses (2) *take to the sky to avoid the predators. A* Chialingosaurus (3) *kicks up dust in a defensive gesture as a family of* Mamenchisauruses (4) *leave the water hole.*

was also a good defense against predators such as *Yangchuanosaurus*. This carnivorous theropod was a top predator of Upper Jurassic Asia. It would have preyed on young and sickly sauropods as well as other smaller dinosaurs such as *Chialingosaurus*. This stegosaurid would have been difficult to kill as it had a tail covered in large spikes that it could swing at attackers.

Yangchuanosaurus was only 34 feet (10.4 m) long and weighed around 3.7 tons (3.4 metric tons).

27

1

Crests and Spines

Quietly munching its way through cycads, ferns, and other low-lying plants of Upper Jurassic Asia was a type of stegosaurid with a big difference. This was *Gigantspinosaurus*, and sticking out from its shoulders were a pair of very large, **scythe**-like spines.

Smaller than a *Stegosaurus*, this spiny herbivore had a set of very small plates emerging from its neck and back. At the end of its tail were two pairs of small spikes that it could use defensively. Predators such as

28

A pair of Gigantspinosauruses (2) *are spooked by the sudden appearance of a* Guanlong (1). *A flock of* Pterorhynchuses (3) *fly past the stegosaurids on their way to a river to feed.*

Guanlong may have preyed on these herbivores. An early **tyrannosaurid**, it had an unusual crest on its head that was used for display during mating rituals. Flying above their heads were flocks of *Pterorhynchuses*. These medium-sized pterosaurs had a wingspan of 2.8 feet (85 cm). Like *Guanlong*, they also had a crest used for display purposes.

Gigantspinosaurus grew up to 14 feet (4.3 m) long and weighed around 1 ton (0.9 metric ton).

Animal Listing

Other dinosaurs and animals that appear in the scenes.

Apatosaurus
(pp. 6–7)
Sauropod dinosaur
75 feet (23 m) long
North America

Archaeopteryx
(pp. 20–21)
Bird
1.6 feet (0.49 m) long
Europe

Brachiosaurus
(pp. 6–7)
Sauropod dinosaur
29.5 feet (9 m) long
North America, Europe

Brachypterygius
(pp. 14–15)
Ichthyosaur
8.2 feet (2.5 m) long
Ocean

Camptosaurus
(pp. 10–11)
Ornithischian
dinosaur
26 feet (7.9 m) long
North America

Caypullisaurus
(pp. 14–15)
Ichthyosaur
30 feet (9 m) long
Ocean

Ceratosaurus
(pp. 8–9)
Theropod
20 feet (6 m)
Africa, America, Europe

Chialingosaurus
(pp. 26–27)
Stegosaurid dinosaur
13 feet (4 m) long
Asia

Compsognathus
(pp. 20–21)
Theropod dinosaur
2.3 feet (0.7 m) long
Europe

Dacentrurus
(pp. 22–23)
Stegosaurid dinosaur
26 feet (8 m) long
Europe

Dinheirosaurus
(pp. 24–25)
Sauropod dinosaur
20 feet (6 m) long
Europe

Draconyx
(pp. 22–23)
Iguanodont dinosaur
3.5 feet (1.1 m) long
Europe

Dryosaurus
(pp. 10–11)
Iguanodont dinosaur
14 feet (4.3 m) long
North America

Elaphrosaurus
(pp. 16–17)
Theropod dinosaur
20 feet (6 m) long
Africa

Europasaurus
(pp. 20–21)
Sauropod dinosaur
20 feet (6 m) long
Europe

Gargoyleosaurus
(pp. 10–11)
Ankylosaurid dinosaur
13 feet (4 m) long
North America

Giraffatitan
(pp. 18–19)
Sauropod dinosaur
85 feet (26 m) long
Africa

Goniopholis
(pp. 22–23)
Crocodilian
13 feet (4 m) long
North America,
Europe, and Asia

Guanlong
(pp. 28–29)
Theropod dinosaur
9.8 feet (3 m) long
Asia

Huanhepterus
(pp. 26–27)
Pterosaur
8.2-foot (2.5 m) ws
Asia

Liopleurodon
(pp. 14–15)
Plesiosaur
21 feet (6.4 m) long
Ocean

Mamenchisaurus
(pp. 26–27)
Sauropod dinosaur
82 feet (25 m) long
Asia

Metriacanthosaurus
(pp. 24–25)
Theropod dinosaur
26.2 feet (8 m) long
Europe

Ornitholestes
(pp. 10–11)
Theropod dinosaur
6.8 feet (2.1 m) long
North America

Palaeopteryx
(pp. 10–11)
Theropod dinosaur
2 feet (63 cm) long
North America

Pterorhynchus
(pp. 28–29)
Pterosaur
2.8-foot (0.85 m) ws
Asia

Rhamphorhynchus
(pp. 22–23)
Pterosaur
1.3 feet (4.1 m) long
Africa, Europe

Saurophaganax
(pp. 6–7)
Theropod dinosaur
36 feet (10.9 m) long
North America

Glossary

allosaurid A member of the family of medium to large carnivorous theropod dinosaurs that includes *Allosaurus*.

ammonite An extinct marine animal with a shell that looks similar to today's nautilus.

ankylosaurid Member of the *Ankylosaurus* family of armored, plant-eating dinosaurs.

aquatic Living in water.

bivalves Aquatic animals that have two hinged shells, such as clams, oysters, mussels, and scallops.

carnivore Meat-eating animal.

crocodilian Group including crocodilians and their extinct relatives.

cycad A kind of palm.

fossils The remains of living things that have turned to rock.

herbivore Plant eater.

ichthyosaur Sea reptile resembling a dolphin.

iguanodonts Members of the *Iguanodon* family of plant-eating dinosaurs.

juvenile An individual that has not yet reached its adult form.

mass extinction event A large-scale disappearance of species of animals and plants in a relatively short period of time.

ornithischian A member of the bird-hipped, beaked, herbivorous dinosaurs.

paleontologist A scientist who studies the forms of life that existed in earlier geologic periods by looking at fossils.

plesiosaur Marine reptiles with long necks and flippers.

predator An animal that hunts and kills animals for food.

preying Hunting.

pterosaur A flying reptile.

sauropod A member of a group of large plant-eating dinosaurs that had very long necks.

scythe A curve-bladed tool used for cutting crops and grass.

semiarid An area of very little rainfall that can still support some plant life.

stegosaurids A group of herbivorous dinosaurs with plates and spikes along their back and tail.

theropod A member of a two-legged dinosaur family that included most of the giant carnivorous dinosaurs.

tyrannosaurid Member of the *Tyrannosaurus* family of carnivorous theropod dinosaurs.

Index